Niven/Nevin

by Iain Gray

Lang**Syne**

PUBLISHING

WRITING *to* REMEMBER

79 Main Street, Newtongrange,
Midlothian EH22 4NA
Tel: 0131 344 0414   Fax: 0845 075 6085
E-mail: info@lang-syne.co.uk
www.langsyneshop.co.uk

Design by Dorothy Meikle
Printed by Printwell Ltd
© Lang Syne Publishers Ltd 2022

All rights reserved. No part of this publication may be reproduced, stored or introduced into a retrieval system, or transmitted in any form or by any means (electronic, mechanical, photocopying, recording or otherwise) without the prior written permission of Lang Syne Publishers Ltd.

ISBN 978-1-85217-791-1

Niven/Nevin

MOTTO:
Where there is life there is hope
and
Touch not the cat bot (without) a glove
(MacIntosh)

CREST:
A palm branch
and
A wildcat
(MacIntosh)

TERRITORY:
Ayrshire and Galloway

NAME variations include:
MacNevin
McNiven

Chapter one:

The origins of popular surnames

by George Forbes and Iain Gray

***If you don't know where you came from, you won't know where you're going** is a frequently quoted observation and one that has a particular resonance today when there has been a marked upsurge in interest in genealogy, with increasing numbers of people curious to trace their family roots.*

Main sources for genealogical research include census returns and official records of births, marriages and deaths – and the key to unlocking the detail they contain is obviously a family surname, one that has been 'inherited' and passed from generation to generation.

No matter our station in life, we all have a surname – but it was not until about the middle of the fourteenth century that the practice of being identified by a particular surname became commonly established throughout the British Isles.

Previous to this, it was normal for a person to be identified through the use of only a forename.

But as population gradually increased and there were many more people with the same forename, surnames were adopted to distinguish one person, or community, from another.

Many common English surnames are patronymic in origin, meaning they stem from the forename of one's father – with 'Johnson,' for example, indicating 'son of John.'

It was the Normans, in the wake of their eleventh century conquest of Anglo-Saxon England, a pivotal moment in the nation's history, who first brought surnames into usage – although it was a gradual process.

For the Normans, these were names initially based on the title of their estates, local villages and chateaux in France to distinguish and identify these landholdings.

Such grand descriptions also helped enhance the prestige of these warlords and generally glorify their lofty positions high above the humble serfs slaving away below in the pecking order who had only single names, often with Biblical connotations as in Pierre and Jacques.

The only descriptive distinctions among the peasantry concerned their occupations, like 'Pierre the swineherd' or 'Jacques the ferryman.'

Roots of surnames that came into usage in England not only included Norman-French, but also Old French, Old Norse, Old English, Middle English, German, Latin, Greek, Hebrew and the Gaelic languages of the Celts.

The Normans themselves were originally Vikings, or 'Northmen', who raided, colonised and eventually settled down around the French coastline.

They had sailed up the Seine in their longboats in 900AD under their ferocious leader Rollo and ruled the roost in north eastern France before sailing over to conquer England in 1066 under Duke William of Normandy – better known to posterity as William the Conqueror, or King William I of England.

Granted lands in the newly-conquered England, some of their descendants later acquired territories in Wales, Scotland and Ireland – taking not only their own surnames, but also the practice of adopting a surname, with them.

But it was in England where Norman rule and custom first impacted, particularly in relation to the adoption of surnames.

This is reflected in the famous *Domesday Book*, a massive survey of much of England and Wales, ordered by William I, to determine who owned what, what it was worth and therefore how much they were liable to pay in taxes to the voracious Royal Exchequer.

Completed in 1086 and now held in the National Archives in Kew, London, 'Domesday' was an Old English word meaning 'Day of Judgement.'

This was because, in the words of one contemporary chronicler, "its decisions, like those of the Last Judgement, are unalterable."

It had been a requirement of all those English landholders – from the richest to the poorest – that they identify themselves for the purposes of the survey and for future reference by means of a surname.

This is why the *Domesday Book*, although written in Latin as was the practice for several centuries with both civic and ecclesiastical records, is an invaluable source for the early appearance of a wide range of English surnames.

Several of these names were coined in connection with occupations.

These include Baker and Smith, while Cooks, Chamberlains, Constables and Porters were to be found carrying out duties in large medieval households.

The church's influence can be found in names such as Bishop, Friar and Monk while the popular name of Bennett derives from the late fifth to mid-sixth century Saint Benedict, founder of the Benedictine order of monks.

The early medical profession is represented by Barber, while businessmen produced names that include Merchant and Sellers.

Down at the village watermill, the names that cropped up included Millar/Miller, Walker and Fuller, while other self-explanatory trades included Cooper, Tailor, Mason and Wright.

Even the scenery was utilised as in Moor, Hill, Wood and Forrest – while the hunt and the chase supplied names that include Hunter, Falconer, Fowler and Fox.

Colours are also a source of popular surnames, as in Black, Brown, Gray/Grey, Green and White, and would have denoted the colour of the clothing the person habitually wore or, apart from the obvious exception of 'Green', one's hair colouring or even complexion.

The surname Red developed into Reid, while

Blue was rare and no-one wanted to be associated with yellow.

Rather self-important individuals took surnames that include Goodman and Wiseman, while physical attributes crept into surnames such as Small and Little.

Many families proudly boast the heraldic device known as a Coat of Arms, as featured on our front cover.

The central motif of the Coat of Arms would originally have been what was sometimes borne on the shield of a warrior to distinguish himself from others on the battlefield.

Not featured on the Coat of Arms, but highlighted on page three, are the family motto and related crest – with the latter frequently different from the central motif.

Adding further variety to the rich cultural heritage that is represented by surnames is the appearance in recent times in lists of the most common names found throughout the United Kingdom of ones that include Khan, Patel and Singh – names that have proud roots in the vast sub-continent of India.

Echoes of a far distant past can still be found in our surnames and they can be borne with pride in commemoration of our forebears.

Chapter two:

Warfare and witchcraft

A rich and heady brew of the bloodlines of ancient Britons and Irish warrior kings flows through the veins of bearers of the Niven name today.

What became their Scottish heartland of Ayrshire and Galloway was from the fifth century to approximately 1030 one of the core territories of the Brittonic Kingdom of Strathclyde, known in the Cumbric tongue as *Teyrnas Ystrad Clut*.

Known by the Welsh as *Hen Ogledd* – the Old North – this sprawling kingdom embraced northern England and southern Scotland and was also known as *Alt Clut*, from a Brittonic term for the fortress of Dumbarton Rock, the main powerbase.

Having developed during the post-Roman period, it was originally home to the Brythonic tribe the Damnonii and appears to have become known as 'Strathclyde' – the 'strath' or 'valley' of the (River) Clyde – when its centre of power shifted to what is now the Govan area of Glasgow following the sacking of Dumbarton Rock by the Vikings in 870 A.D.

The gene pool of those who would later adopt the Niven name – in spelling variants including Nevin and MacNevin – was added to through migrations from across the Irish Sea to Scotland's western seaboard of the descendants of Cuimhim.

He, in turn, was of the kin of Cian, son of the second century A.D. Irish warrior king of the province of Munster, Olioll Olum.

Adding further lustre to the Niven pedigree is that Cian was married to Sabia, a daughter of one of the most heroic and colourful figures in the annals of Ireland's long saga.

This is the gloriously named Conn of the Hundred Battles, known in Irish-Gaelic as *Conn Céthchathach*, Ard Rí, or High King of Ireland from about 177 to 212 A.D.

In the now redundant form of 'Nevinus' and in this case referring to a forename, a certain Nevinus, a parson of some long-forgotten small Ayrshire parish, is recorded as witnessing a grant to the abbots of Paisley in 1230.

But the Nivens, in this case in the form of 'Nevin', step more clearly onto the pages of Scotland's frequently turbulent historical record more than sixty five years later, in 1296.

This was when a Patrick Fitz (of) Nevin appended his signature to an infamous document.

In July of that year, the Scots had risen in revolt against the imperialist designs of England's King Edward I, known to posterity as the 'Hammer of the Scots'.

But, following his crushing of the rising led by the freedom fighter William Wallace, he brought the entire nation under his subjugation little less than a month later, garrisoning strategic locations and demanding the signing of a humiliating treaty of fealty.

Reluctantly ascribed to at Berwick by 1,500 Scottish earls, bishops and burgesses, the parchment is known as the *Ragman Roll* because of the profusion of ribbons that dangle from the seals of the signatories – among whom was Patrick Fitz Nevin.

The fact that his name appears indicates that he was considered influential enough in Scottish affairs to be required to do so.

The historical record is silent on the matter, but in common with many others who had been forced to sign the roll, it is likely he redeemed himself by taking up arms in defence of Scotland's freedom and independence under the great warrior king Robert the Bruce.

Lending credence to this is that his heartland of Ayrshire was one with which Bruce had been familiar since childhood – and Nevin may well have been a tenant of the Bruces, owing them loyalty and service, particularly through their powerful position as earls of Carrick.

Bruce was enthroned as king at Scone in March of 1306 and over the next eight years experienced defeats that included the battle of Methven in June of 1306 and the battle of Dalrigh, near Tyndrum, Perthshire in August of that year.

But despite these initial defeats and other setbacks, he achieved a stunning series of victories over the occupying English forces that include the battle of Glen Trool, fought on his home turf of the Southern Uplands of Galloway in April of 1307 and the battle of Loudoun Hill, in Ayrshire, the following month.

This latter battle, featured in the 2018 historical action film *Outlaw King*, with actor Chris Pine in the role of Bruce, was a particularly significant victory – laying as it did the groundwork for tactics that would be successfully employed in his triumph over King Edward II at the battle of Bannockburn in 1314.

Away from the battlefield and in a later century but in no less grimmer times, Kate Nevin –

whose name also appears in some accounts as 'Neving' and 'McNiven' in 1715 became one of the last witches to be burned in Scotland and the last in Perthshire.

Her date of birth is not known, but she has been described as 'young' when she served as a nurse to the House of Inchbrakie, in the parish of Monzie, near Crieff, and was well known to the local villagers as a 'healer and prophetess'.

But she lived in dangerous times, with Europe in the grip of witchcraft mania – particularly in Scotland where up to 1,500 persons, 75% of them women, were burned at the stake between the early sixteenth and mid-eighteenth centuries.

A Witchcraft Act was passed in Scotland in 1563, making witchcraft or even consulting with an alleged witch a capital crime, while King James VI added fuel to the flames of persecution with the publication in 1597 of *Daemonologie*, his discourse on the Devil, demons, warlocks and witches.

Healers and prophets such as Kate Nevin were easy prey for the incredulous, who believed 'magical' gifts such as hers must have been bestowed by selling her soul to the Devil – more familiarly known as 'Auld Nick'.

The hysteria against witches and the fact that

Kate, having hailed originally from Strathearn, was perceived as an outsider by the God-fearing folk of Monzie and this fatally culminated in her being accused of witchcraft.

Legend holds she fled into hiding in a cave beside the Shaggy Burn, a stream near the village, where she managed to evade her persecutors for three weeks.

Captured and subjected to a rudimentary trial, she was found guilty and sentenced to suffer 'by fire and faggot', on a site near Monzie Castle.

But before being consigned to the flames, she cursed both the Laird of Monzie, head of the House of Inchbrakie, and the village itself.

In Scotland up to 1,500 people were burned at the stake between the early sixteenth and mid-eighteenth centuries.

Cursing the laird and his heirs, she prophesied: *From father to son, Monzie shall never pass; no heir of line shall ever hold the lands now held by him.*

Fortunately, however, the prophecy did not come to pass, although it was one the family were always aware of and doubtless caused them many a sleepless night.

Kate Nevin's ashes have long since been scattered to the winds, but she is not forgotten, her legacy surviving on the landscape around Monzie in the form of Nevin's Cave, the Kate Nevin Ghost Tree and the Nevin Stone – said to mark the very spot where she was burned to death.

Also known to some residents of the village to this day is the mysterious rhyme:

As long as the Shaggie rins crookit and bent
There'll be a Witch o' Mon-ie
And she'll ne'er be kent.

Meanwhile, although the Nivens have their own proud motto 'Where there is life there is hope' and crest featuring a palm leaf, as kinsfolk of Clan MacIntosh they are also entitled to share theirs – with 'Touch not the cat bot (without) a glove' the motto and the crest a wildcat.

Chapter three:

Mathematics and medicine

Far from the warfare and witchcraft of earlier centuries, bearers of the Niven name have gained recognition through a range of decidedly more constructive endeavours and pursuits, including three Scottish brothers who gained particular acclaim.

Born in 1851 in Peterhead, Aberdeenshire, James Niven was the mathematician and physician who played a key role in helping to combat the Spanish Flu pandemic of 1918 to 1920 that claimed millions of lives.

Graduating with a Master of Arts (MA) degree from Aberdeen University and later gaining one in mathematics from Cambridge University in 1870, he decided to train in medicine at St Thomas' Hospital, London and qualified as a physician in 1880.

A succession of positions followed, including medical officer at the Deptford fever and smallpox hospital – gaining experience that held him in good stead when he tackled the problem of other infectious diseases.

As Medical Officer for Health for the English city of Oldham, he campaigned for tuberculosis to be classed as a notifiable disease and for a time studied in Germany under Robert Koch, discoverer of the TB bacillus in 1882 and one of the main founders of the modern discipline of bacteriology.

Showing an interest well ahead of his time, Niven specialised at Oldham General Infirmary with cases of typhus, smallpox, measles, whooping cough and scarlet fever.

To reduce the incidence of these diseases, he pioneered improvements in the town's standard of housing, water supply, refuse and sewage disposal and reductions in smoke pollution.

It was initiatives such as these, including 'isolation' of infected people, which he later implemented through his role of Medical Officer for Manchester during the Spanish flu pandemic.

Known as the HINI influenza A virus and lasting from February of 1918, just a few months before the end of the First World War, until April of 1920, it infected in four successive waves about 500 million people and claimed a death toll estimated at up to 50 million.

Although commonly known as 'Spanish flu', the first recorded cases and deaths were actually in the USA, France, Germany and Britain.

But, to maintain wartime morale in all these nations, censors downplayed early reports of cases – while newspapers were free to report an outbreak in neutral Spain, including the serious illness of King Alfonso III.

This served to focus attention on Spain, leading to the pandemic being dubbed 'Spanish flu'.

Studies have since shown the viral infection had been exacerbated by factors including wartime malnourishment, poor hygiene and overcrowded hospitals and military medical camps – something which at the time had already resonated with the expert on infectious diseases James Niven.

He accordingly tightened up on preventive measures such as the ones that had already been implemented in both Oldham and Manchester – making him the first medical officer in Britain to do so.

Observing the much smaller death toll in these cities compared to others, Niven's measures were gradually adopted by other local authorities and are considered to have contributed to a significant reduction in cases and mortality.

In common with the Covid-19 pandemic that began to sweep the world from the early months of 2020, statistics also played a vital role in tracking its locations and progress – and this is where Niven's expertise as a mathematician also played a key part.

President of the Epidemiological Section of the Royal Society of Medicine, he retired in 1922, only to tragically take his own life three years later.

Suffering from depression, he took an overdose and swam out to sea at Douglas, on the Isle of Man.

The recipient of awards including an honorary degree from his old alma mater Aberdeen University and the Royal Institute of Public Health, he is featured in the 2018 television documentary *The Flu that Killed 50 million* and which was re-broadcast in 2020 as a timely reminder during the Covid-19 outbreak of the devastating impact of pandemics.

His older brother Charles Niven, born in 1845 in Peterhead, was the mathematician and physicist who wrote ground-breaking works on mechanics, electricity and heat.

Studying mathematics at Aberdeen University, where he later spent most of his career and, in common with his brother, Cambridge University, he was responsible for establishing the physics department at Marischal College, Aberdeen, when it was founded in 1909.

A Fellow of the scientific think-tank the Royal Society and honorary member of the Edinburgh Mathematical Society, he died in 1923.

He was also a brother of the mathematician and electrical engineer Sir William Davidson Niven, born in 1842.

In common with his brothers, he was also educated at Aberdeen and Cambridge universities and, in 1882 was appointed director of studies at the Royal Naval College, Greenwich.

A colleague of James Clerk Maxwell, he edited the Scottish mathematical physicist's papers following his death in 1879 while one of his students was the English mathematician and philosopher Alfred North Whitehead; he died in 1917.

Still in the cerebral realms of mathematics, but on North American shores, Ivan Morton Niven was the Canadian-American mathematician renowned for his pioneering work on number theory.

Born in 1915 and a professor for a time at the University of Oregon, he died in 1999.

President of the Mathematical Association of America, he gives his name to discoveries on number theory including Niven's Numbers, Niven's Theorem and Niven's Constant, while the asteroid *12513 Niven* is named in his honour.

On Australian shores and with the Niven spelling variant 'Nevin', Thomas Nevin was the pioneering photographer recognised as the first to work with the police in Australia.

Born in Tasmania in 1842, in addition to his work as a commercial photographer – taking pictures of happy family groups and the scenic wonders of his native island – he also undertook work on behalf of the police for identification photographs of prisoners.

In a career spanning from the early 1860s to the later 1880s he took hundreds of 'mug shots' of prisoners that are the earliest of their kind to survive in public collections.

These include the Tasmanian Museum and Art Gallery, Hobart, the Queen Victoria Museum in Launceston, Tasmania, the State Library of New South Wales, Sydney and the National Library of Australia, Canberra.

Also held in private collections throughout the world, they have been described as "strikingly beautiful, with the expressions and poses of the prisoners allowing us a window into the lives of these men".

Thomas Nevin died in 1923 and it was not until nearly 55 years later, in 1977, that they were exhibited for the first time in public.

This was at the Queen Victoria Museum in Launceston, with the then curator John McPhee commenting: "These photographs are among the most moving and powerful images of the human condition... you can sense the emotions of these long-deceased spirits.

"Their presence is represented as a ghostly imprint on the golden surface of this vast and beautiful land."

Chapter four:

On the world stage

Born at Belgravia Mansions, London in 1910, James David Graham Niven was the award-winning actor and best-selling writer better known as David Niven.

His father William was of Scottish descent and his grandfather hailed from the Perthshire village of St Martin's, while his mother was of Welsh and French ancestry.

Contrary to his birth certificate that he was born in London, Niven nevertheless frequently claimed that he had been born a year earlier than stated, in the Scottish village of Kirriemuir, Angus.

There is no doubt he was proud of his Scots roots, one indication of which is that after graduating from the Royal Military Academy, Sandhurst, in 1930 with a commission as a second lieutenant, he requested he be assigned to a Scottish regiment.

But, he stressed, this should not be to the Highland Light Infantry because, unlike other Scottish regiments such as the Black Watch (Royal Highland Regiment), they wore trews instead of kilts.

Request denied he was duly assigned to the

trews-wearing Highland Light Infantry where, despite promotion to lieutenant in 1933, he did not exactly endear himself to his commanding officers.

Impatient that he might miss a dinner date with a young lady because of a lengthy presentation he was undergoing on machine guns, when asked at the end of the lecture if he had any questions he replied: "Could you tell me the time, sir? I have to catch a train."

Placed under close arrest for insubordination, he and the fellow officer guarding him polished off a bottle of whisky and Niven made his escape through a window.

He then promptly quit British shores for the United States and resigned his commission by telegram while crossing the Atlantic.

Settling in New York City, a brief succession of jobs followed including whisky salesman, before heading for Hollywood and attracting the attention of film producers – not least because of his 'officer and a gentleman' persona.

A number of small parts followed until producer Samuel Goldwyn spotted him in the 1936 *Mutiny on the Bounty* and signed him to the contract that truly launched his career.

Screen credits from this period include the 1936 *The Charge of the Light Brigade*, starring beside his friend Errol Flynn, the 1937 *The Prisoner of Zenda* and, co-starring with Ginger Rogers, the 1939 *Bachelor Mother*.

Returning to Britain after the outbreak of the Second World War and recommissioned as a lieutenant in the Rifle Brigade (Prince Consort's Own) and later with the Commandos, he was assigned to a training base in the West Highlands.

Serving with a reconnaissance and signals unit in France following the D-Day landings in June of 1944, on one occasion when leading his nervous men into action he told them: "Look, you chaps only have to do this once. But I'll have to do it all over again. In Hollywood with Errol Flynn!"

Returning to Hollywood after the war, screen credits throughout the 1950s include *The Moon is Blue*, *Carrington V.C.* and *Around the World in 80 Days*, while he received the Academy Award for Best Actor for his role of an army major in the 1958 *Separate Tables*.

Throughout the 1960s, memorable credits include *The Guns of Navarone*, *55 Days at Peking* and as James Bond in the 1967 *Casino Royale*, while later films include the 1978 *Murder on the Orient Express*.

As a writer, success came with his 1971 autobiography *The Moon's a Balloon*, followed four years later with his Hollywood reminiscences *Bring on the Empty Horses*.

But along with success came tragedy.

His first wife, Primula "Primmy" Niven, whom he had married in wartime London in 1940, died six years later, aged only 28, after fracturing her skull in an accidental fall in the home in Hollywood of the actor Tyrone Power, while she and other guests had been playing a game of hide and seek.

He died in 1983, while he was the father of the contemporary British film producer and script writer **David Niven Jr.**, born in 1942.

A former executive at Paramount Pictures and Columbia Pictures, films he has produced include the 1976 *The Eagle Has Landed* and, from 1979, *Escape to Athena*, while he was the recipient of a Primetime Emmy Award in 1985 as executive producer of *The Night They Saved Christmas*, which he also co-wrote.

From 1993 until their divorce in 1998, he was married to the American actress **Barbara Niven** (née Buchotz), born in 1953 in Portland, Oregon and whose screen credits include the role of Marilyn Monroe in the 1998 HBO film *The Rat Pack*.

In the world of the written word, **John Niven** is the Scottish author born in 1968 in Irvine, Ayrshire.

Having worked for a time in the music industry, his first book was the 2005 *Music from Big Pink*, while his 2008 novel *Kill Your Friends*, a satire on the music industry, was hailed by *Word* magazine as "possibly the best British novel since *Trainspotting*."

Other novels include the 2011 *Second Coming* and the 2018 *Kill 'em All*, while along with Nick Ball, brother of television presenter Zoe Ball, he also pens screenplays.

On American shores, Laurence van Cott Niven is the award-winning science fiction writer better known as **Larry Niven**, born in Los Angeles in 1938.

Author of works including the 1970 *Ringworld*, the cult classic that has gathered awards including a Nebula and a Hugo and the series *The Magic Goes Away*, he is also known for his 'Niven's Laws' which include:

> *Giving up freedom for security is*
> *beginning to look naïve*

and, rather more flippantly:

> *Never fire a laser at a mirror*

In a different writing genre, **Jennifer Niven**, born in 1968 in Charlotte, North Carolina, is the American author best known for her 2015 *All the Bright Things*, winner of a Goodreads Choice Award for Best Young Adult Fiction and also for her series of historical novels including *Becoming Clementine*.

Bearers of the Niven name have also excelled in the highly competitive world of sport.

Born in 1964, **Peter Niven** is the retired jump jockey in National Hunt Racing who holds two rather unusual records.

Winning his first race at Sedgefield in 1984 and becoming a professional jockey two years later, major races he went on to win include the International Hurdle in 1987, the Great Yorkshire Chase in 1991 and 1994 and, in 1997, the Midlands Grand National.

His records were reached at the time of his retirement in 2001 when he became the first Scotsman – having ridden 1,002 winners – to ride more than 1,000 winners and the only jockey to have won five races in a day on four separate occasions.

The recipient of the Lester Award: Jump Jockey of the Year 1991 and the Jump Jockey Special Recognition Award 2000, he is now a racehorse trainer.

On the football pitch and with the Niven

spelling variant 'Nevin', Patrick Kevin Francis Michael Nevin is the Scottish former winger born in Glasgow in 1963 and better known as **Pat Nevin**.

Having played for Scottish clubs Clyde, Kilmarnock and Motherwell and English teams Chelsea, Everton and Tranmere Rovers, he earned 28 caps over a ten-year period playing for his nation.

An inductee of the inaugural Clyde FC Hall of Fame, a former chief executive of his old club Motherwell and now a popular football pundit, he is also a cousin of the English retired footballer Terry Butcher.

From sport to the much different world of art, **Margaret Graeme Niven** was the acclaimed British painter of landscapes, flowers and portraits born in 1906 in Marlow, Buckinghamshire.

A member of esteemed bodies including the Royal Institute of Oil Painters and the Royal Society of British Artists, she died in 1997.

One bearer of the Niven name who found fame through literally unearthing discoveries, **William Niven** was the Scottish mineralogist and archaeologist born in 1850 in Bellshill, North Lanarkshire.

Immigrating to the United States when aged 29 having already established a reputation in mining and mineralogy, it was while on expedition in Llano County, Texas in 1889 that he discovered the three new minerals *yttrialite*, *thorogummite* and, later named for him, *nivenite*.

The expedition, meanwhile, had been undertaken on behalf of the inventor Thomas Edison in search of the mineral *gadolinite*, used as a filament in street lamps.

On a later expedition to Mexico, he discovered the mineral *aguilarite* – but it was also during this visit that his interest in archaeology was aroused.

In 1921, in an area that now forms part of north-western Mexico City, he unearthed a number of tablets bearing mysterious symbols.

Now known as the Niven Tablets, neither Niven himself not anyone else has been able to definitively explain their meaning.

In Niven's lifetime, they became the subject of controversy when the British occult writer, engineer and inventor James Churchward claimed the symbols proved the existence of a long-lost highly advanced race, the Naacals, whose vanished homeland, somewhere in the Pacific Ocean was known as Mu.

Author of the 1926 *The Lost Continent of Mu: Motherland of Man*, Churchward asserted the

Naacals had a number of 'satellite' civilisations, such as those of the Aztecs and Mayas of Mexico, who received the benefit of their knowledge.

Aspects of this ancient wisdom, he claimed, were represented symbolically on the Niven Tablets.

Whatever the truth of the matter, William Niven died in 1937 – while there is an interesting genealogical footnote to his story.

He was the second son of eight children and one of his younger brothers, Forrest, born in 1862 and an artist, had a daughter, Margaret Niven, born in 1898.

Tracing the rather tangled web of the family tree further, we find that Margaret, an actress, married an Ulric van den Bogaerde, born of Flemish ancestry in 1892 in Birmingham.

Ulric died in 1972 and his wife eight years later, while the elder of their two sons was a certain Derek Niven van Bogaerde – born in 1921 and better known to posterity as the late and highly acclaimed British actor Dirk Bogarde.